MEGA MACHINES
EXCAVATORS

D0825728

Amanda Askew

QEB

Quarto is the authority on a wide range of topics.

Quarto educates, entertains and enriches the lives of our readers—enthusiasts and lovers of hands-on living.

www.quartoknows.com

Copyright © QEB Publishing 2016

First published in the US in 2016
by QEB Publishing

Part of The Quarto Group
6 Orchard, Lake Forest, CA 92630

All rights reserved. No part of this publication may be reproduced, stored in a retrieval system, or transmitted in any form or by any means, electronic, mechanical, photocopying, recording, or otherwise, without the prior permission of the publisher, nor be otherwise circulated in any form of binding or cover other than that in which it is published and without a similar condition being imposed on the subsequent purchaser.

A CIP record for this book is available from the Library of Congress.

ISBN 978 1 68297 145 1

Printed in China

Picture credits
Key: t = top, b = bottom, r = right, l = left, c = center

Cover image: Getty Images narvikk, **Alamy Images** David Bagnall 17, Mike Dobel 18–19, David R. Frazier Photolibrary Inc 2b, 21t; **Getty Images** Javier Larrea 3, 10–11, Gary Moon 2t, 9b, 23bl, Liam Bailey 15b, 23br; **iStockphoto LP** Purdue9394 4–5, sonny 2962 12, Shaun Dodds 10tl, 23tr, Sascha Rosenau Njaa 14–15; **RWE** 20–21; **Shutterstock** Four Oaks 1, maggee 6–7, 24b, lvto 4, RGtimeline 7, Jiri Slama 3, 8–9, 23tc, 24t, Sevda 4, Shaun Wilson Link 12–13, MartinMojzis 10b, Maria Jeffs 13c; Joseph S.L. Tan Matt 16–17, 23bc

CONTENTS

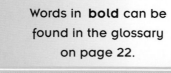

Words in **bold** can be found in the glossary on page 22.

MEET THE EXCAVATORS

Excavators are used to dig holes and trenches. They often work on **construction sites** with other big machines like **backhoe loaders** and **bulldozers**.

Backhoe loaders on wheels can travel by road to get from one job to another.

Some excavators have wheels. Other excavators run on tracks. Tracks stop the excavator from sinking into the ground.

This excavator is called a **crawler**. Its tracks help it move over rough ground.

tracks

PARTS OF AN EXCAVATOR

There are three main parts to an excavator—a cab, an arm, and an **attachment**. The attachment is usually a **bucket** with teeth.

driver's cab

tracks

arm

The driver controls the excavator from the cab.

bucket

The excavator's giant arm joins the bucket or other attachment to the cab.

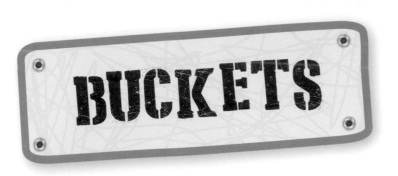

BUCKETS

At the end of the excavator's arm is the bucket. Buckets are made of metal, and come in different shapes and sizes.

The teeth on a bucket come in different sizes, too. Longer, sharper teeth can break through hard surfaces, such as rock.

teeth ↘

Some buckets are very wide. The driver uses a wide bucket to scrape up earth or stones.

A wide bucket can collect lots of stones in each scoop.

HARD WORK

Excavators need special attachments to break through hard ground and to pick things up. There's an attachment for almost every job!

ripper

grapple

A **ripper** looks like a tooth, and is used for digging. A **grapple** can grab and move objects. A **breaker** can break up rock and concrete.

breaker

DIGGING AND CARRYING

grab

The excavator is a busy machine on a construction site. It digs up the ground, and clears any unwanted **rubble** and waste.

The grab clamps together to lift and hold the load.

A **grab** is like two buckets that clamp together. It is used to lift and carry heavy objects, such as piles of rocks.

This excavator is using a grab to recycle cars at a junk yard.

13

DEMOLITION

The excavator driver controls which way the building falls down.

Excavators can be used to knock down houses and small office blocks. This is called demolition. Excavators can **demolish** buildings safely, one bit at a time.

To demolish tall buildings, the excavator uses its long arm to reach up to the top of the building.

Some excavators can reach up to 328 feet (100 meters) in height —that's taller than the Statue of Liberty!

CLEARING WASTE

A vacuum excavator has a powerful hose to suck up waste. It can be used to remove soil from a hole, or water following a flood, or even from a swimming pool.

A vacuum excavator is also useful for cleaning **sewage pipes**.

This machine works like a vacuum cleaner to suck up tons of waste sand.

The air speed in a vacuum excavator's hose may be up to 220 miles (350 kilometers) per hour. That's faster than a Ferrari!

MINING

steel ropes

Excavators are used in mining specially to dig out **coal**. This excavator is a dragline excavator. It drags its bucket along the ground to collect the coal.

Steel ropes are used to move the bucket. One of the ropes moves the bucket up and down. Other ropes move it from side to side.

The bucket empties the coal into trucks to be taken away.

bucket

19

ALL SHAPES AND SIZES

Excavators come in all shapes or sizes depending on the job they do.

giant blades

This mini-excavator can dig deep in tight spots.

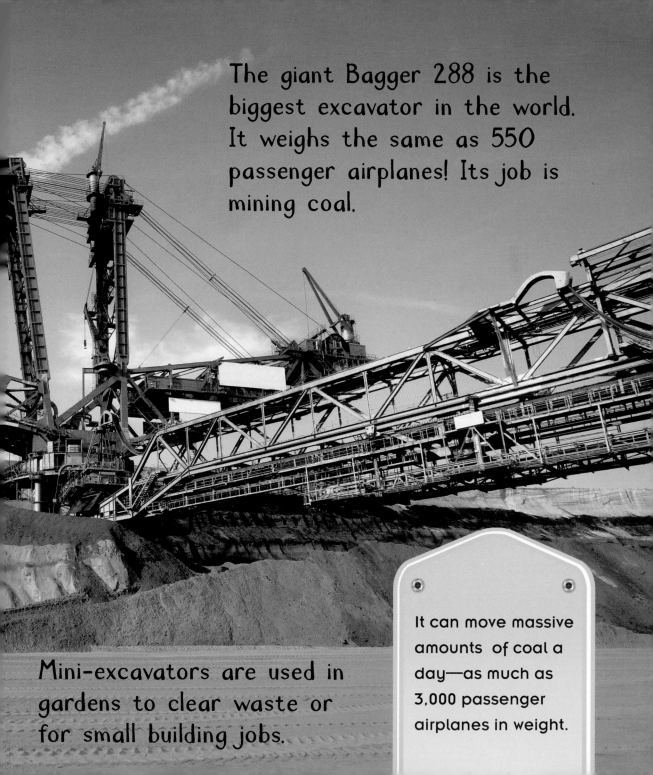

The giant Bagger 288 is the biggest excavator in the world. It weighs the same as 550 passenger airplanes! Its job is mining coal.

Mini-excavators are used in gardens to clear waste or for small building jobs.

It can move massive amounts of coal a day—as much as 3,000 passenger airplanes in weight.

GLOSSARY

attachment
A tool on the end of an excavator's arm.

backhoe loader
A tractor with a large bucket on the front.

breaker
An attachment on an excavator used to break up hard ground.

bucket
A large container on the end of an excavator's arm.

bulldozer
A machine with a blade on the front.

construction site
A place where a house or other building is being built.

crawler
An excavator with tracks to help it move over rough ground.

coal
A hard, black rock that is dug out of the ground.

demolish
To knock down a building.

grab
An attachment that looks like two buckets clamped together.

grapple
An attachment on an excavator used for moving objects.

ripper
An attachment used for digging in hard ground.

rubble
Broken stones or brick.

sewage pipe
A pipe that takes waste away from buildings.

EXCAVATOR FUN

1 Look back through the book to find these three attachments. What does each one do?

2 Which is the biggest excavator in the world?

3 Which machine on a construction site would you like to operate? Why?

4 Which picture below shows a vacuum excavator?

5 Look out for excavators at work on a construction site. What jobs were they doing? What color were they? Draw a picture.

INDEX